Living or Nonliving?

by Abbie Dunne

CAPSTONE PRESS
a capstone imprint

Pebble Plus is published by Capstone Press,
1710 Roe Crest Drive, North Mankato, Minnesota 56003
www.mycapstone.com

Library of Congress Cataloging-in-Publication Data
Names: Dunne, Abbie, author.
Title: Living or nonliving? / by Abbie Dunne.
Description: North Mankato, Minnesota : Capstone Press, [2017] | Series:
  Pebble plus. Life science | Audience: Ages 4-8.? | Audience: K to grade
  3.? | Includes bibliographical references and index.
Identifiers: LCCN 2016005320 | ISBN 9781515709428 (library binding) | ISBN
  9781515709749 (pbk.) | ISBN 9781515711094 (ebook pdf)
Subjects: LCSH: Life (Biology)--Juvenile literature. | Organisms--Juvenile
  literature.
Classification: LCC QH309.2 .D86 2017 | DDC 570--dc23
LC record available at http://lccn.loc.gov/2016005320

Editorial Credits
Linda Staniford, editor; Bobbie Nuytten, designer; Jo Miller, media researcher;
Tori Abraham, production specialist

Photo Credits
Shutterstock: Andresr, 5, ArTDi101, 9, BGSmith, 11, Bruce MacQueen, 13, Dave Allen Photography, 19, Dennis
van de Water, 17, Eric Isselee, cover, Mny-Jhee, 1, Ozgur Coskun, 21, Richard A McMillian, 7, Shevs, 15

Design Elements
Shutterstock: Alena P

Note to Parents and Teachers

The Life Science set supports national curriculum standards for science. This book introduces
the concept of living or nonliving. The images support early readers in understanding the
text. The repetition of words and phrases helps early readers in understanding the text. This
book also introduces early readers to subject-specific vocabulary words, which are defined in
the Glossary section. Early readers may need assistance to read some words and to use the
Table of Contents, Glossary, Read More, Internet Sites, Critical Thinking Using the Common
Core, and Index sections of the book.

Printed and bound in China. PO5151

Table of Contents

Living or Nonliving?

The world is full of life.

Take a deep breath! You are

a living human being.

Look around! Plants and

animals are living things too.

There are also many nonliving things in the world. A ball and a bicycle are not alive. Rocks, sand, and water are nonliving things too.

Energy

Living things need energy.

Plants make energy from sunlight,

air, and water. They catch sunlight

on their leaves. Water and air enter

the plant through its leaves and roots.

Animals need energy too.
They eat food for their bodies
to make energy. Animals also
drink water and breathe air
to survive.

Moving and Reacting

Living things move on their own. Nonliving things cannot move on their own. Plants shoot up from the soil. Animals walk, run, fly, or swim.

Living things react
to things around them.
Plants react by bending
toward sunlight. Animals
react with their senses.

Growing and Reproducing

Living things reproduce. They
make more of their own kind.
Ducks lay eggs. Ducklings
grow up to be like their parents.
Nonliving things cannot reproduce.

Living things grow and change.

Leaves grow and change color.

Then they fall to the ground.

All living things grow old and die.

Activity

The world is full of living and nonliving things. Find out how to tell the difference between them.

What You Need

- pencil and paper
- area to survey

What You Do

1. Make a table on a sheet of paper. It could look like this one. Add numbers to 20.

THING	ACTIONS	LIVING	NONLIVING
1.			
2.			
3.			
4.			
5			

2. Pick 20 things you see around you.

3. In the Actions column, write down what each thing is doing on its own, or what you have seen it do on its own over time. If a thing does not do anything on its own, leave the Actions column blank.

4. Decide if the thing is living or nonliving. Put a check in that column.

What Do You Think?

Make a claim.

What is one way to tell the difference between living and nonliving things?

Use the results of your experiment to find out.

Glossary

energy—the strength to do active things

living—alive

nonliving—not alive; not having the qualities of living things

react—to act in response to something that happens

reproduce—to make offspring

root—the part of a plant that is underground

senses—seeing, hearing, tasting, smelling and touching; using our senses helps us learn about our surroundings

survive—to stay alive

Read More

Braun, Eric. *Gertrude and Reginald the Monsters Talk About Living and Nonliving.* In the Science Lab. North Mankato, MN: Picture Window Books, 2012.

Rissman, Rebecca. *Living and Nonliving in the Mountains.* Is It Living or Nonliving? Chicago: Raintree, 2013.

Spilsbury, Louise. *What are Living and Nonliving Things?* Let's Find Out: Life Science. New York: Britannica Educational Publishing in association with Rosen Educational Services, 2014.

Internet Sites

FactHound offers a safe, fun way to find Internet sites related to this book. All of the sites on FactHound have been researched by our staff.

Here's all you do:

Visit *www.facthound.com*

Type in this code: 9781515709428

Check out projects, games and lots more at
www.capstonekids.com

Critical Thinking
Using the Common Core

1. Name four things that a living thing needs to stay alive. (Key Ideas and Details)

2. Living things react to changes around them. What do you think this means? (Key Ideas and Details)

3. Is a tree living or nonliving? How do you know? (Integration of Knowledge and Ideas)

4. Do you think a toy car is a living or nonliving thing? (Integration of Knowledge and Ideas)

Index